China's Growing Risk Tolerance in Space

People's Liberation Army Perspectives and Escalation Dynamics

HOWARD WANG, GREGORY GRAFF, ALEXIS DALE-HUANG

Prepared for the Department of the Air Force
Approved for public release; distribution is unlimited.

RAND PROJECT AIR FORCE

For more information on this publication, visit **www.rand.org/t/RRA2313-2**.

About RAND

RAND is a research organization that develops solutions to public policy challenges to help make communities throughout the world safer and more secure, healthier and more prosperous. RAND is nonprofit, nonpartisan, and committed to the public interest. To learn more about RAND, visit www.rand.org.

Research Integrity

Our mission to help improve policy and decisionmaking through research and analysis is enabled through our core values of quality and objectivity and our unwavering commitment to the highest level of integrity and ethical behavior. To help ensure our research and analysis are rigorous, objective, and nonpartisan, we subject our research publications to a robust and exacting quality-assurance process; avoid both the appearance and reality of financial and other conflicts of interest through staff training, project screening, and a policy of mandatory disclosure; and pursue transparency in our research engagements through our commitment to the open publication of our research findings and recommendations, disclosure of the source of funding of published research, and policies to ensure intellectual independence. For more information, visit www.rand.org/about/research-integrity.

RAND's publications do not necessarily reflect the opinions of its research clients and sponsors.

Published by the RAND Corporation, Santa Monica, Calif.
© 2024 RAND Corporation
RAND® is a registered trademark.

Library of Congress Cataloging-in-Publication Data is available for this publication.

ISBN: 978-1-9774-1346-8

Cover: Li He/Xinhua/Alamy Live News.

Limited Print and Electronic Distribution Rights

This publication and trademark(s) contained herein are protected by law. This representation of RAND intellectual property is provided for noncommercial use only. Unauthorized posting of this publication online is prohibited; linking directly to its webpage on rand.org is encouraged. Permission is required from RAND to reproduce, or reuse in another form, any of its research products for commercial purposes. For information on reprint and reuse permissions, please visit www.rand.org/pubs/permissions.

About This Report

Chinese leaders see themselves in competition with the United States to build military power in space. The multiplication of U.S. and Chinese capabilities could lead to unstable competition in space, raising the risk of rapid, and perhaps unintended, military escalation. This report surveys open-source literature across the Chinese defense enterprise to present a composite image of People's Liberation Army (PLA) perspectives and key factors for U.S.-China crisis stability in space. It draws on authoritative Chinese writings to understand Chinese perceptions of threats from the United States by reviewing Chinese publications on U.S. intent and capabilities in space. The report additionally traces the evolution of PLA thinking on escalation dynamics in space over the past two decades. The report concludes with an assessment of the challenges facing U.S. officials looking to manage U.S.-China crisis dynamics in space. The other publicly available volumes in the series are as follows:

- Alexandra T. Evans, Andrew Radin, Katie Feistel, Krista Langeland, Bruce McClintock, and Howard Wang, *Space Strategic Stability: Assessing U.S. Concepts and Approaches*, RAND Corporation, RR-A2313-1, 2024.
- Cheyenne Tretter, *Exploring Factors for U.S.-Russia Crisis Stability in Space*, RAND Corporation, RR-A2313-3, forthcoming.

The research reported here was commissioned by Headquarters, U.S. Space Force, Chief Strategy & Resourcing Officer (CSRO) and conducted within the Strategy and Doctrine Program of RAND Project AIR FORCE as part of a fiscal year 2023 project, "Crisis Stability in Space."

RAND Project AIR FORCE

RAND Project AIR FORCE (PAF), a division of RAND, is the Department of the Air Force's (DAF's) federally funded research and development center for studies and analyses, supporting both the United States Air Force and the United States Space Force. PAF provides the DAF with independent analyses of policy alternatives affecting the development, employment, combat readiness, and support of current and future air, space, and cyber forces. Research is conducted in four programs: Strategy and Doctrine; Force Modernization and Employment; Resource Management; and Workforce, Development, and Health. The research reported here was prepared under contract FA7014-22-D-0001.

Additional information about PAF is available on our website:

www.rand.org/paf/

This report documents work originally shared with the DAF on August 28, 2023. The draft report, dated October 2023, was reviewed by formal peer reviewers and DAF subject-matter experts.

Acknowledgments

The authors would like to thank Gen Jay Raymond for approving the overall research project, as well as Stephen Hart and Col Elvert Gardner for supporting the RAND-proposed project structure, including this report. At RAND, conversations with Bruce McClintock, Andrew Radin, Alexandra Evans, Krista Langland, Edward Geist, and Nathan Beauchamp-Mustafaga provided insight into the current debates and dilemmas that shape U.S. policy and improved our understanding of several concepts. We are also grateful to PAF Strategy and Doctrine Program director Raphael Cohen and to the report's reviewers, Kristen Gunness and Dean Cheng, for their thoughtful suggestions.

We are grateful to the U.S. officials who shared their time and insights on the choices confronting the U.S. space community. All errors or omissions remain the sole responsibility of the authors.

Summary

Issue

Chinese leaders see themselves in competition with the United States to build military power in space. The ongoing development of U.S. and Chinese capabilities could lead to unstable competition in space, raising the risk of rapid, and perhaps unintended, military escalation.

Approach

This report surveys open-source literature across the Chinese defense enterprise to present a composite image of People's Liberation Army (PLA) perspectives and key factors for U.S.-China crisis stability in space. It draws on authoritative Chinese writings to understand Chinese perceptions of threats from the United States by reviewing Chinese publications on U.S. intent and capabilities in space. The report additionally traces the evolution of PLA thinking on escalation dynamics in space over the past two decades. We assess the challenges facing U.S. officials looking to manage U.S.-China crisis dynamics in space.

Key Findings

The analysis in this report yielded the following findings:

- Chinese leaders perceive a global trend in which China is in the process of replacing the United States as the world's dominant power. In this perspective, the United States is a dominant but declining power that is likely to lash out against rising powers and implement strategies to extend its status by undermining Chinese development, including by inflating the threat of China as a pretext for militarization across domains, including in space.
- Authoritative PLA literature makes clear that space deterrence, like all PLA deterrence, contains both deterrent and compellent elements, ultimately meant to coerce an enemy into submission to Beijing's political objectives. The literature informs the PLA's established escalation ladder, up to and including the use of lethal force. The PLA's approach to deterrence and escalation in space prioritizes securing political objectives over avoiding conflict. Beijing could initiate conflict activities if it judged the political risk of inaction to be greater than the military risk.
- Chinese leaders harbor deep suspicions of the United States and begin with an assumption of both great malice and great capability when assessing threats posed by the United States in space. As a result of these suspicions, Chinese leaders have inflated perceptions of U.S. threats and adopted a policy approach that resists cooperating with the United States to arrest unintended crisis escalation.

- Contemporary PLA research is significantly more risk tolerant than authoritative PLA professional military education published in 2013, which was likely generated prior to Xi Jinping's term as the Chinese Communist Party (CCP) General Secretary. Research published since 2013 emphasizes Xi's guidance to be more proactive in shaping the international environment, including by accepting higher but carefully calibrated levels of risk of unintended escalation.

Implications and Recommendations

The findings in this report suggest key implications for the U.S. government, the joint force, and the U.S. Space Force (USSF):

- PLA researchers see crisis communications mechanisms as leverage-bearing tools. Because Chinese leaders view the United States as prosecuting hegemony-maintaining strategies against China, Chinese leaders tend to interpret U.S.-led efforts to establish crisis communications mechanisms or broader space norms as tools to control China's behavior. Therefore, Chinese leaders claim that it is not in China's interest to engage in such efforts with the United States.
- Without the direct means for arresting unintended crisis escalation in space, U.S. officials responsible for managing U.S.-China crises in space will likely need to adapt to compressed decision cycles with little communication to achieve a version of stability that Chinese leaders will tolerate. Moreover, U.S. officials will likely need to do so without expectations of cooperation with the PLA.
- U.S. officials should avoid investing costly efforts or making significant policy concessions to establish crisis communications mechanisms with the PLA. Given the CCP's history of aversion to crisis communications with the United States, PLA overtures to discuss such mechanisms might not be made in good faith. Nor are communications mechanisms focusing on safety likely to be upgraded into crisis communications mechanisms affecting security. Instead, such overtures will likely be efforts to bait the United States into sinking time and energy into endless negotiations.
- The PLA's push to proactively shape its strategic environment indicates that USSF will face a bellicose PLA eager to assert itself in space during peacetime, although the PLA remains unlikely to escalate in a way that risks its political imperatives. USSF should anticipate that PLA provocations in peacetime likely comprise a new normal in day-to-day space operations that involve China.
- Still, the PLA's proactive steps and higher risk tolerance remain subordinate to political decisionmaking. In interpreting PLA messaging, USSF operators should anticipate that the PLA is not likely to take proactive, escalatory steps in a crisis if those steps undermine its ability to prosecute such politically imperative missions as a war over Taiwan. Though PLA operators might consider the space domain sufficiently stable for escalatory actions, they might not view political circumstances to be as permissive.

Contents

Tables

Chapter 1

Introduction

Chinese leaders see themselves in competition with the United States to build military power in space. The ongoing development of capabilities and doctrine for space operations in both countries might reveal a growing risk of unintended military escalation in space. Central to this risk is each country's threat perception of the other, or how it assesses the other's intentions and its capabilities to act on those intentions. Additionally, guidance from each country's defense enterprise on how to respond to crises and control escalation will shape escalation dynamics in the event of a crisis or conflict. In other words, the risk of unintended military escalation in space between the United States and China turns on whether each country views the other as a threat in space and how it will respond to that threat.

This report surveys open-source literature across the Chinese defense enterprise to present a composite image of People's Liberation Army (PLA) perspectives and key factors for U.S.-China crisis stability in space.[1] It draws on authoritative materials, including leader speeches reported in official media, defense white papers, and official professional military education (PME), which collectively reflect political leader guidance or PLA strategy and doctrine. Although PLA PME through 2020 is publicly available, the PLA's most authoritative materials on space are more than a decade old. To address this gap, this report draws on open-source research published by scholars in China's major PME institutions, such as the Academy of Military Science (AMS), National Defense University (NDU), and National University of Defense Technology (NUDT), to approximate likely developments in PLA thinking on space over the past decade. This report also draws from research by PLA service members working on space issues, particularly in former PLA Strategic Support Force (SSF) billets. The report begins with a brief overview of the importance of space power in China's national strategy under Chinese Communist Party (CCP) General Secretary Xi Jinping. From there, it proceeds in two broad sections. The first section reviews PLA publications on U.S. intent and capabilities in space to arrive at a characterization of threat to CCP strategic objectives. The second section traces the evolution of PLA thinking on escalation dynamics in space from 2000 through the early 2020s. The report concludes with an assessment of challenges facing U.S. officials looking to manage crisis dynamics in space.

---

[1] This report examines PLA perspectives, not capabilities, in space. For assessments on China's space capabilities, see Defense Intelligence Agency, *Challenges to Security in Space: Space Reliance in an Era of Competition and Expansion*, 2022; Kari A. Bingen, Kaitlyn Johnson, Makena Young, and John Raymond, *Space Threat Assessment 2023*, Center for Strategic and International Studies, 2023; Brian Weeden and Victoria Samson, eds., *Global Counterspace Capabilities: An Open Source Assessment*, Secure World Foundation, 2023.

Space and the Chinese Dream

Space power is a critical component of the CCP's vision for China's national rejuvenation. CCP leaders have repeatedly called on party members and the Chinese populace to work toward "realizing the Chinese Dream of the great rejuvenation of the Chinese nation," a loosely defined goal characterized by securing a preeminent position for China in any global order.[2] Xi has personally linked the ideas of national rejuvenation and the Chinese Dream with a subordinate "Space Dream," extending the amorphous requirements of China's preeminence into the space domain. In a 2013 call with Chinese astronauts, for example, Xi asserted that "the Space Dream is an important component of the dream of [becoming] a strong country."[3] Similarly, when announcing the inaugural "China Space Day" in 2016, Xi expounded, "exploring the vast cosmos, developing the space industry, and building China into a space power is China's eternal dream."[4]

Space power in CCP thinking cannot be separated from military power. The 2013 *Science of Military Strategy* published by the PLA's AMS referred to the space domain as the "commanding heights" housing "indispensable strategic supports for winning informationized wars."[5] China's 2019 Defense White Paper calls space a "critical domain in international strategic competition."[6] The 2020 *Science of Military Strategy* published by PLA's NDU is more explicit about the role of space as a warfighting domain that interlinks with other domains. It argues, "in the context of the new military revolution, space has already become a new domain of military conflict, not only changing the traditional form of warfare of mankind, but also expanding the struggle for national strategic interests."[7] Similar values appear to guide the China Aerospace Science and Technology Corporation (CASC), the state-owned enterprise serving as the primary contractor for China's space program. In a 2022 article published in the CCP Central Committee journal *Party Building* [党建], CASC Party Secretary and Chairman Wu Yansheng emphasized the corporation's work in space will forever serve its "chief responsibility of strengthening [China's] military," with two discrete goals.[8] Wu announced that by 2030, CASC will be a world-class space enterprise to support China's national defense and military modernization, and by 2045, CASC will support China's construction of a world-class

---

[2] Communist Network [共产党员网], "1. Realizing the Chinese Dream of the Great Rejuvenation of the Chinese Nation" ["一、实现中华民族伟大复兴的中国梦"], undated; Nadège Rolland, *China's Vision for a New World Order*, National Bureau of Asian Research, 2022; Daniel Tobin, "How Xi Jinping's 'New Era' Should Have Ended U.S. Debate on Beijing's Ambitions," testimony before the U.S.-China Economic and Security Review Commission hearing on *A 'China Model'? Beijing's Promotion of Alternative Global Norms and Standards*, March 13, 2020.

[3] Wu Yansheng [吴燕生], "Guided by General Secretary Xi Jinping's Important Exposition on Building China into a Space Power, Strive to Write a New Chapter in the Development of China's Space Industry" ["以习近平总书记关于建设航天强国重要论述为指引 奋力谱写航天事业发展新篇章"], *Party Building* [党建], June 21, 2022.

[4] "Xi Jinping Earnestly Entrusts the Task of Building China into a Space Great Power," Xinhua, April 12, 2019.

[5] Shou Xiaosong [寿晓松], ed., *Science of Military Strategy*, Academy of Military Science Press, 2013, p. 96.

[6] State Council Information Office [国务院新闻办公室], *China's National Defense in the New Era* [新时代的中国国防], July 24, 2019.

[7] Xiao Tianliang [肖天亮], ed., *Science of Military Strategy (2020 Edition)*, [战略学 (2020 年修订)], National Defense University Press [国防大学出版社], 2020, p. 142.

[8] Wu, 2022.

military and promote China's comprehensive development into a world-class space power.[9] To achieve China's national rejuvenation, CCP leaders and China's space enterprise believe China must dominate—and dominate militarily—in space.

CCP leaders see their space ambitions in the context of strategic competition with a technologically superior United States. CCP propaganda claims that the defining trend of the global international system is a deep, long-term adjustment, which CCP officials often characterize as "the East is rising, and the West is falling." According to this claim, the United States remains the dominant but declining global power in the near term, and it attempts to resist systemic trends undermining its hegemony by suppressing potential competitors, such as China.[10] Moreover, in this view, space power is one of the emerging sources of national power and a critical means by which the United States will attempt to maintain its global hegemony.[11] PLA authors extend this logic to U.S. commercial and foreign partnerships in space, viewing them as tools by which the United States will boost its own military space power and coerce or limit China's development of space power.[12] Chinese defense publications reveal broad suspicion of U.S. intentions in space, exhibiting enduring views that the United States has consistently sought to weaponize and maintain superiority in space across administrations to ensure its own global hegemony.[13]

These suspicions muddle state threat perceptions and can become compelling drivers to inadvertent crisis escalation. A threat is composed of a prospective adversary's intentions and their capabilities.[14] Given the enduring CCP perspectives of a rapacious United States intent on suppressing China's national rejuvenation demonstrated in the "East is rising, West is falling" slogan, CCP leaders almost certainly harbor intense suspicions and perceive inflated threats from the historical and ongoing development of U.S. military space capabilities.[15] CCP perspectives of the United States as an adversary are especially prominent in the PLA, which broadly refers to the United States as the "strong enemy."[16] The CCP has held these suspicions of the United States for decades, and they have

---

[9] Ren Changsheng [任长胜] and Deng Yunan [邓雨楠], "CASC Held the 2021 New Employee Initiation Training Opening Ceremony" ["航天科技集团召开 2021 年新员工入职培训开班式"], *China Space News* [中国航天报], August 6, 2021.

[10] See, for example, Tian Peiyan [田培炎], "Deeply Study and Understand Xi Jinping Thought on Socialism with Chinese Characteristics for a New Era" ["深学细悟习近平新时代中国特色社会主义思想"], *People's Daily*, July 4, 2023; Provincial Health Commission of Hubei Province, "'New, Progressive, Real'—Analysis of Key Words in the New Development State" ["'新, 进, 实' 一新发展阶段的关键词浅析"], January 7, 2021.

[11] See Xu Nengwu [徐能武] and Huang Changyun [黄长云], "The Origin, Evolution and Development Trend of Space Arms Control from the Perspective of International Security" ["国际安全视角下太空军控的缘起、演进和发展动向"], *Diplomatic Review* [外交评论], No. 5, 2014; Zhong Jing [仲晶], "Strategic Competition and Games in Space Are Becoming Increasingly Fierce" ["太空战略竞争与博弈日趋激烈"], *Academic Frontiers* [学术前沿], No. 8, 2020.

[12] Xie Shanshan [谢珊珊], Wu Ling [吴灵], and Li Yun [李云], "Research and Analysis of the U.S. National Defense Space Strategy" ["美国《国防太空战略》研究分析"], *Aerospace China* [中国航天], No. 9, 2020.

[13] Fan Gaoyue [樊高月] and Gong Xuping [宫旭平], "The Development and Evolution of American Space Strategic Thought (Part 1)" ["美国太空战略思想的发展与演变(上)"], *National Defense* [国防], No. 2, 2016a; Fan Gaoyue [樊高月] and Gong Xuping [宫旭平], "The Development and Evolution of American Space Strategic Thought (Part 2)" ["美国太空战略思想的发展与演变（下）"], *National Defense* [国防], No. 3, 2016b.

[14] Thomas C. Schelling, *Arms and Influence*, reprint, Yale University Press, 2008, p. 36.

[15] Tian, 2023; Tobin, 2020.

[16] Nathan Beauchamp-Mustafaga, "Dare to Face the 'Strong Enemy 强敌': How Xi Jinping Has Made the PLA Talk About the United States," *Sinocism*, March 4, 2021.

sharpened in recent years under Xi.[17] In a notional future in which CCP leaders' suspicions of U.S. intentions have grown so significant as to become destabilizing and foment crisis, these leaders might experience what Thomas Schelling called the "anxiety to strike first" and trigger inadvertent escalation.[18]

PLA thinking on space conflict strongly suggests the belief that space is offense-dominant, which Schelling considers a key component of the anxiety to strike first in the relevant domain.[19] The PLA's official PME on space operations clearly defines space as an offense-dominant domain. It explicitly describes two dominant trends in the development of space technology: First, space-based capabilities are characterized as "strong on offense and weak on defense," and second, space operational tempo continues to increase and shortens the decision space available to state leaders.[20] In a crisis, anxieties might be exacerbated as PLA decisionmakers weigh their courses of action against what they consider to be a militarily superior United States in a pressure- and time-intensive environment.

Furthermore, the PLA's approach to deterrence—in the space domain and more broadly—appears to emphasize risk-accepting escalation to extract political victories rather than arresting escalation. PLA literature emphasizes deterrence rather than stability in space. In PLA writings, deterrence is a tool to cow an adversary who would otherwise complicate Chinese activities, not an effort to prevent an adversary from destabilizing an environment.[21] Similarly, Chinese concepts of deterrence include compellence, such as coercing another state into taking actions in Beijing's interest.[22] PLA authors are explicit that deterrence is not strictly a tool for de-escalating crisis or averting conflict, and some level of conflict is acceptable. AMS literature describes successful space deterrence as "breaking the enemy's resistance without fighting or with minimal fighting."[23] How the PLA conducts its deterrence operations in a crisis will be critical for understanding the prospects for U.S.-China crisis stability. Moreover, how the PLA's approach to deterrence and escalation changes as its perceptions of U.S. threats in space evolve will likely shape the PLA's behavior in avoiding or exacerbating unintended escalation during a crisis in space.

---

[17] Tobin, 2020; Beauchamp-Mustafaga, 2021.

[18] Thomas C. Schelling, "Confidence in Crisis," *International Security*, Vol. 8, No. 4, Spring 1984, p. 56.

[19] Schelling, 1984, p. 56.

[20] Jiang Lianju [姜连举], ed., *Lectures on the Science of Space Operations* [空间作战学教程], Military Science Press [军事科学出版社], 2013, pp. 35, 73.

[21] Academy of Military Science All-Military Military Terminology Committee [全军军事术语管理委员会 军事科学院], *Junyu* [军语], Academy of Military Science Publishing House [军事科学出版社出版], 2011, pp. 5, 51, 58.

[22] Nathan Beauchamp-Mustafaga, Derek Grossman, Kristen Gunness, Michael S. Chase, Marigold Black, and Natalia D. Simmons-Thomas, *Deciphering Chinese Deterrence Signalling in the New Era: An Analytic Framework and Seven Case Studies*, RAND Corporation, RR-A1074-1, 2021, p. viii.

[23] Jiang, 2013, p. 126.

Chapter 2

Chinese Perceptions of U.S. Strategy and Military Capabilities for Space

This section has three components, all of which review recent PLA scholarship on U.S. space capabilities and policy and find PLA researchers express deep suspicions of the United States and begin their threat assessments of the United States with assumptions of both great malice and great capability. Although none of the reviewed scholarship is authoritative PLA policy or doctrine, research by leading experts in the PLA reveal some of the trends of thought leaders who are most influential for shaping how the PLA continues to understand the United States. Openly published PLA scholarship is not comprehensive; politically sensitive topics or reexaminations of key military assessments are likely to have limited distribution within the CCP or PLA information systems.

The first component examines the PLA's views on the U.S. intentions driving U.S. space strategies, highlighting PLA interpretations of the 2020 Defense Space Strategy as a naked effort to seize "space hegemony." The second component assesses the PLA's research into U.S. space capabilities, including a focused examination into the Schriever wargames. This component reveals a PLA tendency to overestimate the United States' capabilities and processes for developing new capabilities. The third component focuses on PLA writings on U.S. commercial and foreign partnerships in space, finding that PLA researchers consistently interpret these agreements as efforts to boost U.S. military power or curtail the PLA.

PLA Perceptions of U.S. Space Strategy and Intent

PLA analyses of U.S. strategic approaches to space at the national level tend toward worst-case assumptions of U.S. intent, often assessing broadly consistent strategic goals across administrations to weaponize space and preserve U.S. hegemonic advantages. Two of the PLA's dedicated scholars on U.S. strategy, Air Force Command Academy Department of Strategic Operations [空军指挥学院战略战役系] Assistant Professor Colonel Gong Xuping and AMS Foreign Military Research Department [军事科学院外国军事研究部] Head Expert [首席专家] Senior Colonel (ret.) Fan Gaoyue wrote a notable example in a two-part series reviewing the space strategies of every U.S. president from Dwight D. Eisenhower to Barack Obama. This article presented the development of the U.S. space program as racing to establish military hegemony in space. According to these authors, the Eisenhower administration sought to develop military space applications under the cover of civilian applications, the Carter administration sought to ban anti-satellite systems while developing such systems, and the George W. Bush administration pursued "absolute space superiority" and was the first to deploy weapons in space.[24] Notably, these articles were published in 2016, prior to the period of heightened U.S.-China competition seen during the Trump and Biden administrations.

After 2016, PLA authors began highlighting the injection of competition-focused language within U.S. national space strategic documents and policies.[25] This body of research by PLA academics appears to view U.S. space policy as forming a discrete policy system for containing China in space. PLA NDU Professor Zhong Jing, for example, emphasized in a 2020 article how successive U.S. administrations have used strategies, regulations, and policy guidelines as "top-level design" of U.S. space power.[26] Another two professors with the PLA NUDT separately assessed that the United States has, through a series of strategic documents, established a relatively complete "policy system" for controlling outer space and promoting its weaponization in service to a U.S. space strategy to seize the "commanding heights" of military competition.[27]

PLA Perceptions of the 2020 Defense Space Strategy

More recent PLA analysis has particularly emphasized the Trump administration's 2020 Defense Space Strategy, which PLA writers characterize as blatantly securing and extending U.S. "space hegemony."[28] Leading PLA researchers appear to disagree on the drivers of the 2020 strategy. One camp argues that the United States is formulating new space policies because it perceives a greater threat to its military dominance in space.[29] Another argues instead that continued U.S. development of space capabilities has brought the United States to a culminating point, where it is able to assert even greater ambitions in space than it could prior.[30] Neither opinion contains any self-reflection on how PLA capabilities in space might be perceived by the United States and generate the impetus for a U.S. defense space strategy in response.

Several PLA researchers appear to believe that the 2020 Defense Space Strategy reveals anxieties over U.S. perceptions of China's developing space capabilities. One set of PLA researchers associated with the NUDT and the Joint Logistics Support Force (JLSF) concluded that the United States views China's and Russia's development of space forces as threats, and U.S. anxieties about the loss of global

---

[24] Fan and Gong, 2016a; Fan and Gong, 2016b.

[25] Although PLA authors' assessments of U.S. space policy intensified their focus on competition-focused language, PLA assessments of U.S. intentions in space did not fundamentally change in response to the United States. As demonstrated in the prior paragraph, PLA researchers consistently view U.S. administrations as seeking "absolute superiority" or "hegemony" in space, in alignment with the CCP's broader assessment that the United States is and has been attempting to arrest its decline. PLA authors might have viewed such developments as the 2018 National Defense Strategy using competition language for the first time as confirming or intensifying their assessments, but even prior to 2016, PLA authors consistently viewed U.S. policy with suspicion or hostility.

[26] Zhong, 2020.

[27] Xu and Huang, 2014.

[28] Fan and Gong, 2016a; Fan and Gong, 2016b.

[29] See, for example, Long Kun [龙坤], Zhu Qichao [朱启超], Chen Xi [陈曦], and Ma Ning [马宁], "The Motivation, Characteristics and Influence of the Trump Administration's Space Defense Strategy Adjustment" ["特朗普政府太空防卫战略调整的动因，特点与影响"], *National Defense Technology* [国防科技], Vol. 42, No. 4, 2021.

[30] See, for example, Xie, Wu, and Li, 2020.

space superiority make the "temptation" to weaponize outer space "inevitable."[31] These researchers are careful to also argue that U.S. concerns are baseless, and the authors minimize U.S. assessments of China's counterspace capabilities—such as its anti-satellite missile test in 2007—as exaggerations.[32] Another set of researchers affiliated with the NUDT and Hunan Institute of Technology similarly assessed the 2020 Defense Space Strategy as driven by a "strong awareness of opponents and a strong sense of urgency" while attempting to maintain a "leading position" for the United Space in space, suggesting that the United States is working to develop new military capabilities in space out of fear of what it perceives to be an eroding margin of military superiority over China and Russia.[33]

Other PLA researchers take the opposite position, claiming the 2020 Defense Space Strategy is merely the natural next step taken by a sober United States that has reached a new stage in its development of space capabilities. In a 2020 article, researchers with the PLA SSF Space Systems Department [战略支援部队航天系统部] assessed that, in accordance with the scope, strategic background, and organizational positioning of the strategy within the hierarchy of U.S. strategic documents, the release of the 2020 strategy means that "the U.S. space combat readiness has entered the stage of systematic advancement."[34] The authors offer four predictions of U.S. space strategy as a result of their perceived systemic advancement. First, the United States will seek to consolidate and maintain its space hegemony by further cultivating "comprehensive space strength." Second, the United States will emphasize developing its space forces' policy, strategy, operations, investment, capabilities, and professional skill set toward space warfighting. Third, the United States will draw on commercial assets and allied space forces to augment its existing space military capabilities. Fourth, the U.S. military will use the newly established U.S. Space Force (USSF) and U.S. Space Command to further seize comprehensive space superiority.[35]

PLA Perceptions of U.S. Space Capabilities

PLA scholarship on U.S. space capabilities often assume outstanding U.S. capability development and an elevated threat to CCP interests, typically with very little evidence and threadbare reasoning. PLA researchers examining U.S. capabilities often draw implications for China's broader strategic and nuclear balance, for example, but the researchers very rarely provide clear, rigorous rationale or evidence for how that space capability negatively affects China's strategic deterrence. A 2021 article written by PLA researchers affiliated with the PLA NDU provides a notable example. The authors assessed that the U.S. military's increased use of satellite internet would undermine a presently

[31] Long et al., 2021.

[32] Long et al., 2021.

[33] The authors assess that the U.S. Democratic Party and Republican Party share a common goal of maintaining global hegemony, including in space, but the two parties adopt different means of achieving this shared end. According to these writers, Democrats look to maintain U.S. space hegemony through multilateral partnerships, while Republicans seek to do so through unilateral coercion (Su Feng [粟锋] and Xu Nengwu [徐能武], "Countermeasures and Developmental Trends of the US Defense Space Force Based on the Interpretation of the US *Defense Space Strategy* in 2020" ["美国国防太空力量发展的动向及应对—基于对美国 2020 年《国防太空战略》的解读"], *National Defense Technology* [国防科技], Vol. 42, No. 3, 2021).

[34] Xie, Wu, and Li, 2020.

[35] Xie, Wu, and Li, 2020.

balanced situation of international strategic deterrence.[36] According to these authors, the deployment of large numbers of communication satellites in orbit would extend the U.S. military's nuclear situational awareness globally, improving the speed, accuracy, and survivability of U.S. nuclear forces and "break[ing] the current pattern of strategic deterrence balance."[37] Yet the authors cite as their only evidence the 2018 Nuclear Posture Review, which stated that the U.S. Department of Defense (DoD) would update its strategic early warning, command and control, and communication systems to create a more efficient and stable strategic deterrent system.[38]

Similarly, another group of researchers with the NUDT and JLSF asserted that because U.S. space deterrence policy does not rule out attacking the space assets of potential opponents, U.S. offensive space operations risk triggering nuclear war, with the assumption that major powers would necessarily regard an attack on satellites as a prelude to an attack on nuclear forces.[39] The authors offer no considerations of whether attacked countries are able to distinguish between satellites necessary for nuclear command and control versus others, nor whether attacks are reversible or irreversible. This pattern of worst-case thinking driven by only loosely specified mechanisms for how space conflicts escalate pervades much of the reviewed literature and almost certainly indicates an analytic skew in PLA scholarship toward exaggerating the threat that U.S. space capabilities pose to any potential adversary. Notably, the PLA's analytic skew toward catastrophizing is consistent with CCP political guidance. Xi Jinping has publicly directed China's national security apparatus to insist on "worst-case thinking" in preparation to withstand the "perils of major trials."[40]

PLA scholars' published assessments of U.S. military space organizations often imagine, with little evidence, that the United States enjoys development of new space capabilities. For example, researchers from PLA Unit 63611, an SSF unit based at the Korla Missile Test Complex in Xinjiang,[41] assessed that U.S. Space Training and Readiness Command's (STARCOM's) "training system" is "very sound, and the training content is substantial and complete" on the basis that STARCOM has organizations dedicated to space training, doctrine development, wargaming, and education, as well as in-place training and testing.[42] Similarly, another group of NUDT researchers assessed that USSF has straightforward tasks of researching, developing, and deploying new space

---

[36] Chen Yunlei [陈云雷], Li Xianglong [李向龙], and Wang Xinxin [王鑫鑫], "Research on the Trend of Military Application of Satellite Internet in the United States and Its Impact" ["美国卫星互联网军事应用趋势及其影响研"], *Aerodynamic Missile Journal* [飞航导弹], No. 2, 2021.

[37] Chen, Li, and Wang, 2021.

[38] Chen, Li, and Wang, 2021.

[39] Long et al., 2021.

[40] "Xi Jinping Presides Over the First Meeting of the 20th Central National Security Commission and Emphasizes Accelerating the Modernization of a National Security System and Capabilities Such That a New Security Pattern Safeguards the New Development Pattern," Xinhua, May 30, 2023.

[41] PLA units use five-digit cover designators to mask the specific identity of a unit writing in public. Analysts can infer information about the unit from other factors. Publications by Unit 63611 regularly locate the unit in the city of Korla in Xinjiang at postal code 841000, which is dominated by the Korla Missile Test Complex operated by the SSF. See, for example, Yin Hang [尹航], Guo Su [郭谡], Wen Chaoran [温超然], Yang Chuang [杨闯], and Bi Peng [毕鹏], "Analysis of Development of US MALD and Coping Strategies" ["美微型空射诱饵武器发展分析与应对策略"], *Air & Space Defense* [空天防御] Vol. 2, No. 3, 2019, p. 84.

[42] Guo Wenbo [苟文波], Luo Wei [罗威], and Bi Chenglong [毕成龙], "Analysis of U.S. Space Training and Readiness Command" ["美军太空训练与战备司令部浅析"], *Aerospace China* [中国航天], No. 11, 2022.

weapons; developing and verifying new space combat concepts; and carrying out space operations as needed. The authors do not consider any potential challenges USSF might face in this predicted development. Moreover, these researchers asserted with little evidence that U.S. military development favors offensive capabilities. The NUDT researchers insisted in their analysis that offensive counterspace operations will be USSF's "primary choice and focus" in force planning and construction, while defensive space operations can be "optimized based on existing space assets," posing an increased overall threat to the space activities of all other countries.[43]

PLA Studies of the Schriever Wargame

PLA academics have used the Schriever Wargame as a locus for analyzing U.S. space capabilities. Studies of the wargame extend across major PLA PME institutions and consistently reveal the PLA impression that the annual wargame serves to accelerate U.S. development of offensive space capabilities to preserve space superiority. The AMS's authoritative PME on space operations claims that the U.S. military organizes the Schriever Wargame series to "enhance its abilities for actual warfare in space operations."[44] NUDT researcher Guo Jun calls it a "military operation to step up preparations for space operations and maintain space superiority."[45] PLA NDU Professor Zhong Jing stated that it is the strategic counterpart of the more tactically oriented Space Flag exercise, and that through the Schriever Wargame series the U.S. military has "further enriched and improved" its space deterrence strategy, space combat doctrine, ability to use space combat power, and approaches to space capabilities development.[46]

NUDT researcher Guo's article is particularly revealing and indicates a tendency among some PLA researchers to overestimate U.S. space capabilities by assuming any capabilities discussed at Schriever Wargame exercises are in the late stages of development or already deployed.[47] In reality, many of these exercises test the effects of proposed or notional capabilities that might not be in a mature stage of development.[48] For example, Guo claimed that in Schriever I, the Blue team used reversible anti-satellite weapons to disable the Red team's satellites, while in Schriever III, the U.S. team used irreversible means. In both examples, Guo tied the activity in the wargame to alleged U.S. space research and development programs, strongly implying the exercised scenarios were likely reflective of U.S. capabilities. Guo further asserted that the United States has tested reversible space weapons as early as 1984, space shuttles *Challenger* and *Discovery* carried out tests of laser and particle beam weapons and that, in 1997, the U.S. military decommissioned weather satellites with ground-based lasers.[49] The latter appears to be referencing a test of the U.S. Army's Mid-Infra-Red Advanced

---

43 Guo, Luo, and Bi, 2022.

44 Jiang, 2013, pp. 7–12.

45 Guo Jun [郭俊], "Viewing the Construction of U.S. Space Deterrent Force from the 'Schriever' Exercise" ["'从施里弗'演习看美军太空威慑力量构建"], *National Defense Science and Technology* [国防科技], Vol. 36, No. 1, February 2015.

46 Zhong, 2020.

47 Guo, 2015.

48 Air Force Space Command Public Affairs, "Schriever Wargame Concludes," Schriever Space Force Base, December 18, 2015.

49 Guo, 2015.

Chemical Laser (Miracl) against an aging satellite to measure the vulnerability of U.S. satellites to laser attack.[50] The former appears to have been a test associated with the development of the Star Wars program that aimed to understand how the atmosphere distorts lasers traveling from the ground into space.[51] With respect to irreversible weapons, Guo asserted that the U.S. military verified space-based kinetic energy weapons—among other programs—through the Brilliant Pebbles and Clementine II missions. The former was a proposal to develop space-based antiballistic missile kinetic kill vehicles that was canceled during the Clinton administration and never succeeded in orbiting a prototype system. The latter was a joint undertaking between the National Aeronautics and Space Administration (NASA) and the Ballistic Missile Defense Organization to repurpose brilliant pebbles technologies in an asteroid impactor role.[52] Altogether, the logic in Guo's assessments of the Schriever wargames hinged heavily on assuming that U.S. space wargames test mature or nearly mature capabilities, the results of which is analysis that systematically overestimates U.S. capabilities.

At least one Chinese author points to the Schriever wargames as a deterrent signal that China should learn from to communicate China's capabilities as a means of strategic signaling and deterrence. Highlighting unspecified instances of reporters' interviews of U.S. officials at Schriever, the author notes that the Department of the Air Force uses these engagements to announce the various space weapons it plans to use, including missile defense systems, anti-satellite lasers, and reusable space planes, all of which are intended to make opponents carefully weigh their ability to strike first against the United States.[53] Notably, PLA PME also considers using public media to display military space forces as a low-intensity deterrent activity meant to be carried out in peaceful times and crisis and in complement with political and diplomatic actions.[54]

PLA Perceptions of U.S. Space Partnerships

A common theme in PLA academic research is the claim that U.S. commercial and foreign partnerships are non-agent tools by which the United States will boost its own military space power and coerce or limit China's power. NDU Professor Zhong Jing asserts that the United States is actively engaged in space cooperation with its allies to build a space alliance, draw allies in by sharing space situational awareness and promises of cooperative development, increase their dependencies on the United States, and ensure that potential opponents cannot use or access the allies' space capabilities.[55] NUDT researcher Xu Nengwu argued that the United States will take advantage of its strong space situational awareness capabilities to exaggerate the seriousness of space debris and together with its allies will seek to "dominate" the formulation of space traffic management rules,

[50] "In Test, Military Hits Satellite Using a Laser," *New York Times*, October 21, 1997.

[51] Thomas O'Toole, "Space Shuttle Succeeds in Laser Test," *Washington Post*, June 22, 1985.

[52] Donald R. Baucom, "The Rise and Fall of Brilliant Pebbles," *Journal of Social, Political and Economic Studies*, Vol. 29, No. 2, Summer 2004.

[53] Wu Ming [吴明] and Ling Shengyin [凌胜银], "Strategic Thinking on Strengthening Our Country's Space Deterrence Capability Construction" ["加强我国太空威慑能力建设的战略思考"], *China Military to Civilian* [中国军转民], No. 2, 2019.

[54] Jiang, 2013, pp. 126–128.

[55] Zhong, 2020.

emphasizing monitoring and regulations that will restrict and suppress the space capabilities of other countries, almost certainly including China, to "asymmetrically counterbalance hegemony."[56] Xu further wrote that alliances in space will become increasingly unreliable for maintaining stability as the strategic significance of space grows, claiming that the United States' weaponization of space, born of hegemonic aspirations, directly threatens the sustainable use of space and damages the interests of such allies as European Union member states. Xu described this hypothesis in contrast to China's and Russia's approaches, which Xu and other Chinese authors characterize as advocating for the non-weaponization of space and the prevention of a space arms race.[57]

Some PLA researchers see similarly bellicose drivers behind DoD's engagement with U.S. commercial space partners. SSF Space Systems Department author Xie Shanshan claims the United States pursues commercial space partners out of a belief that commercial capabilities can ensure that the United States maintains a leading edge in space technology development. Xie assesses that the U.S. military will make full use of commercial cooperation to integrate commercial and military space architectures.[58]

[56] Xu and Huang, 2014.

[57] Xu and Huang, 2014.

[58] Xie, Wu, and Li, 2020.

Chapter 3

PLA Thinking on Escalation Dynamics in Space

From the 2000s through the late 2010s, PLA thinking on escalation—and escalation in space—has shown a growing proclivity toward the use of force and a greater comfort with managing the uncertainty that results from conflict. These trends are visible through an uneven literature composed of the PLA's regularly published PME texts on general strategic issues, irregularly published PLA PME on strategic issues in space, and open-source academic publications from PLA scholars. Authoritative PLA PME on space issues is concentrated in 2013 and otherwise sparse, and analysis of PLA thinking on escalation in space over time requires supplementation from other, less authoritative PLA literature.[59] By setting the contours of PLA thought, authoritative PLA discussion and educational materials on escalation establish the parameters within which PLA thinking on escalation almost certainly developed. Therefore, a close examination of the two in concert can serve as an analytical aid to fill gaps in the PLA's literature on space.

This section first discusses publicly available PLA PME between 2001 and 2013 to serve as an analytic baseline of PLA thought on deterrence and escalation. Next, it turns to PLA PME discussions of space operations and escalation dynamics in 2013 and examines how PLA thought on space fits within the greater landscape of its strategic thought. Third, it provides an overview on how PLA thinking on escalation has evolved between 2013 and 2020. This section also offers a speculative analysis on how PLA discussions on space escalation dynamics have likely evolved between 2013 and 2020 given broader trends in PLA thinking during the same time.

Evolution in PLA Thinking on Deterrence and Escalation, 2001–2013

Since the early 2000s, PLA views on escalation have shifted from sprawling views of peacetime competitive dynamics to take on a tight focus on the application of military force and its likely effects. Successive iterations of the PLA's *Science of Military* Strategy show a PLA in transition from

---

[59] For other examinations of PLA thinking on space, see Nathan Beauchamp-Mustafaga, "Exploring Chinese Thinking on Deterrence in the Not-So-New Space and Cyber Domains," in *Modernizing Deterrence: How China Coerces, Compels, and Deters*, National Bureau of Asian Research, 2023; Alexis A. Blanc, Nathan Beauchamp-Mustafaga, Khrystyna Holynska, M. Scott Bond, and Stephen J. Flanagan, *Chinese and Russian Perceptions of and Responses to U.S. Military Activities in the Space Domain*, RAND Corporation, RR-A1835-1, 2022; Krista Langeland and Derek Grossman, *Tailoring Deterrence for China in Space*, RAND Corporation, RR-A943-1, 2021.

theoretical approaches to escalation and war to more practical considerations of escalation dynamics in a near-term conflict with the United States.[60]

Authoritative PLA thinking on escalation in the early 2000s was largely theoretical and attempted to present a unifying concept of crisis and conflict escalation. The 2001 AMS *Science of Military Strategy* has an expansive discussion of escalation management through the lens of war control [战争控制], which the authors wrote has a sweeping utility for "preventing the occurrence of war, and once war is inevitable . . . controlling its vertical and horizontal escalation . . . to reduce negative consequences or to gain a major victory at minor cost."[61] Other leading analysis of this 2001 discussion noted that it emphasized peacetime efforts to avoid conflict; a contemporary and seminal analysis of PLA war control described it as leveraging all aspects of comprehensive national power to "shape the international environment and make war less likely."[62]

Between 2001 and 2013, PLA strategic thought appeared to undergo a significant transition that pivoted away from peace maintenance and toward military competition or "struggle" [斗争] short of war. This is most clearly demonstrated in the 2013 edition of the *Science of Military Strategy*, which reduces the 2001 edition's chapter-length discussion of war control to a single line: under the 2013 paradigm, war control is "controlling combat intensity" [调控武力] to achieve political objectives through military competition "within the strategic opportunity that exists between total war and total peace" [全面战争与全面和平之间增加新的战略选择].[63] To the PLA in 2013, measured and controlled escalation was desirable if it achieved the objectives set by CCP political leaders; escalation was not inherently undesirable. This assessment is reinforced and clarified by the 2013 *Science of Military Strategy's* discussion of military deterrence, which notes it has a "fundamental goal" to "contain external aggression, prevent a conflict from escalating to war, or implement anti-deterrence against hegemonic-style deterrence."[64] War is still an undesirable outcome to be deterred, but preventing war is not the sole or even primary objective of PLA deterrence. Instead, PLA deterrence has two alternative objectives of containing foreign aggression against Chinese interests and countering U.S. efforts to shape Chinese behavior through its own deterrent activities.[65]

Other 2013 PLA research shows this shift in PLA thinking on escalation might be informed by a more antagonistic—or more openly antagonistic—view of the United States. In a 2013 *China Military Science* article, NDU Crisis Management Center [国防大学危机管理中心] Professors Zhao Ziyu and Zhao Jingfang warned of the inevitability of crisis and conflict with political differences. According to these researchers, "for countries or political organizations with a conflict of fundamental interest, because of the presence of a long-standing grudge and even hostility, if an incident takes place,

---

[60] The *Science of Military Strategy* volumes cited here were published by the PLA AMS in 2001 and 2013 and by the PLA NDU in 2017 and 2020.

[61] Peng Guangqian and Yao Youzhi, eds., *The Science of Military Strategy*, official English-language translation of the 2001 Chinese edition, Military Science Press, 2005, p. 159.

[62] Lonnie D. Henley, "Evolving Chinese Concepts of War Control and Escalation Management," in Michael D. Swaine, Andrew N. D. Yang, and Evan S. Medeiros with Oriana Skylar Mastro, eds., *Assessing the Threat: The Chinese Military and Taiwan's Security*, Carnegie Endowment for International Peace, 2007, p. 86.

[63] Shou, 2013, p. 110.

[64] Shou, 2013, p. 145.

[65] Shou, 2013, p. 145.

hostility between the two countries will escalate to a higher level regardless of the magnitude of the incident" and "military crisis becomes inevitable."[66] Although Zhao and Zhao do not name the United States in their article, the reference to conflicts of fundamental interest strongly implies long-standing PLA views of the U.S.-China relationship that also informed the 2013 *Science of Military Strategy*'s reference to "hegemonic-style deterrence."[67]

A key theme of the 2013 shift in PLA educational materials appears to be that crisis and conflict with the United States cannot be deterred, and PLA deterrence and escalation control must therefore emphasize opposing U.S. efforts to shape China's behaviors rather than simply oppose war. Therefore, escalating a military crisis or conflict short of total war might be a desirable step to achieve CCP political objectives.

PLA Thought on Escalation in Space in 2013

The PLA's leading publicly available PME on space operations, the 2013 *Lectures on the Science of Space Operations*, contains a discussion on escalation dynamics in space that closely parallels the official PME on escalation dynamics broadly and describes offensive actions as deterrents against the United States in a crisis or conflict. Like the other materials published in 2013 that were discussed in the prior subsection, the 2013 *Lectures* tends toward managing a likely if not inevitable crisis by cowing opponents into submission through military competition to safeguard CCP political objectives, which explicitly includes selective military escalation.

Consistent with the argument from NDU Crisis Management Center researchers Zhao and Zhao, the 2013 *Lectures* asserts that long-standing structural factors tend to move space escalation dynamics toward crisis and conflict, which might be inevitable. As noted earlier, in the 2013 *Lectures*, leading PLA space operations theorists assessed that space operations "are strong on offense and weak on defense," and the offense-dominant quality of space will only grow more pronounced as technology continues to advance.[68] Moreover, the authors of the *Lectures* believe that the technological advancements driving what they assessed to be the offense-dominant nature of space will accelerate escalation by compressing decision cycles. Specifically, given improving detection, maneuver, targeting, and strike technologies, "the rhythm of space operations has clearly accelerated, and their processes have clearly been shortened."[69]

Consistent with the 2013 *Science of Military Strategy*'s discussion of deterrence, the 2013 *Lectures* presents a system of space deterrence that prioritizes coercing the opponent into submission to achieve CCP political objectives. The 2013 *Lectures* makes clear that space deterrence, like all PLA deterrence, is compellence meant to cow an enemy into submission. The PLA's theory of the logic of deterrence postulates that having a powerful set of space forces and "threatening to use or actually using limited space forces to awe and contain the opponent's military activities" will demonstrate China's "real

---

[66] Zhao Ziyu [赵子聿] and Zhao Jingfang [赵景芳], "On Control and Management of Military Crises" [论军事危机的管控], *China Military Science* [中国军事科学], No. 4, 2013.

[67] Shou, 2013, p. 145.

[68] Jiang, 2013, p. 73.

[69] Jiang, 2013, p. 35.

strength and resolve," which in turn "generates doubt, fear, and wavering in the enemy and forces him to abandon his operational intention."[70] Although the goal for space deterrence—and deterrence generally—is to "break the enemy's resistance without fighting or with minimal fighting," the principle is one of efficiency rather than conflict aversion. The PLA's concept of deterrence is emphatically about breaking an adversary's will, not necessarily about preventing the outbreak of war.[71]

The 2013 *Lectures* describes a list of space deterrence operations that explicitly include the use of violent force, which some other states might consider an act of war. The textbook describes a four-step escalation ladder for space deterrence operations, shown in Table 3.1.

Table 3.1. PLA Escalation in Space Deterrence Operations

Steps (in order of increasing escalation)	Description
Show of space strength	Well-publicized but low-intensity tests of advanced space equipment; typically accompanying political and diplomatic lines of effort. Can be conducted in peacetime or early stages of a crisis. Examples include technology demonstrations that might be publicized by CCP propaganda outlets, displayed at international exhibitions or seen by invited foreign military observers.
Space military exercises	Demonstrate to the enemy the PLA's capability and resolve for winning a war by displaying the PLA's space posture and war preparations.
Disposition of space forces	Posture space forces for "strategic attack" with the intention of giving the enemy a sense of a "large enemy force bearing down on the border" such that they might abandon their objectionable policies. Primarily entails projecting space forces (e.g., launching and transporting personnel, weapons and equipment, and operational materiel) and readjusting the disposition of PLA space forces (e.g., employing launch, orbital maneuver, and terrestrial maneuver to prepare for space information and firepower operations).
Overawing space strike	Limited scale, initial, and well-targeted strikes on enemy command and control or other vulnerable nodes in enemy system-of-systems. Might entail "soft kill" directed energy or electromagnetic attacks or "hard kill" kinetic strikes. Intended to force an adversary into abandoning their military designs or into signing a "coerced peace treaty."

SOURCE: Features information from Jiang, 2013, pp. 127–128.

[70] Jiang, 2013, p. 126.

[71] Jiang, 2013, p. 126.

These steps leave significant room for misperception.[72] For example, the PLA might conduct its least-escalatory action—the show of space strength—either in peacetime or in the early stages of a crisis. This varied employment muddies the operation's utility as a deterrent signal to other states, which might recognize the PLA's activity as standard peacetime behavior rather than an attempt to deter some activity.[73] Similarly, the 2013 *Lectures* dictates no strict order in which these steps must be taken and offers that they can be "simultaneously employed or conducted without a strict priority," further confusing potential space adversaries with nonstandardized deterrent activities.[74]

Consistent with the 2013 *Science of Military Strategy*'s discussion on war control, the 2013 *Lectures* emphasizes the controllability of space deterrent operations. The *Lectures* assesses space deterrent operations "will become the main form of military deterrence, and the frequency of its use will grow" because of its "strategic quality, convenience, and *controllability*" (emphasis added).[75] This assessment closely aligns with the 2013 *Science of Military Strategy*'s discussion of measured and controlled escalation as a desirable method of force employment. In fact, the principle of war control is manifest in how the *Lectures* describes calibrating the PLA's deterrent operations. To align the PLA's escalatory behavior with political objectives, the *Lectures* instructs the PLA to carefully assess each situation and calibrate its use of offensive force to the current circumstances such that it is neither too high (for fear the adversary will reject the deterrent and "rush ahead into danger") nor too low (for fear the adversary will not feel cowed from its initial objective).[76] In effect, war control in space requires cautious and precise assessments supporting bespoke operations specific to the unique attributes of the particular circumstances of the deterrent operation.

PLA scholars writing in this time frame suggest that the PLA might be more willing to blur the lines between crisis and conflict in its deterrent activities because it perceives comparatively limited consequences in the event deterrence in space fails, particularly if the escalation remains non-kinetic. In 2015, NUDT scholars argued that

> the failure of space deterrence does not have immediate and catastrophic consequences. Soft-kill antisatellite weapons with local effects might generally be used early in a conflict . . . space systems after the Outer Space Treaty onward do not carry nuclear weapons, so attacks on satellites are emphatically not nuclear missions and therefore do not directly threaten humanity.[77]

---

[72] Notably, although the PLA does not appear to acknowledge the possibility that it might misperceive another actor's intentions or signals, the 2013 *Lectures* notes the need for PLA officers conducting space deterrence operations to ensure that their adversaries do not misperceive PLA intentions. The *Lectures* repeatedly emphasizes "adopting the method of gradual escalation," with graduated processes ensuring that deterrent force clearly increases with each successive step and preventing an overescalation such that "the adversary will have difficulty accepting it [and instead] rush ahead into danger" (Jiang, 2013, pp. 127, 130).

[73] Jiang, 2013, p. 127.

[74] Jiang, 2013, p. 127.

[75] Jiang, 2013, p. 126.

[76] Jiang, 2013, p. 131.

[77] Zhou Lini [周黎妮], Fu Zhongli [傅中力], and Wang Shu [王姝], "Comparison Between Space Deterrence and Nuclear Deterrence" ["太空威慑与核威慑比较研究"], *National Defense Science & Technology* [国防科技], Vol. 36, No. 3, June 2015, p. 53.

That is, retaliation might occur and occur outside the space domain, but it will not be overwhelming so long as counterspace operations do not "threaten humanity."[78] The consequences that PLA scholars identify for the failure of space deterrence include the loss of investment in orbital equipment, suspension of security and economic functions served by space systems, and the potential challenges of space debris that result from kinetic strikes in space.[79] Although these PLA scholars do not dismiss the failure of space deterrence as entirely without consequence, the consequences they highlight appear to imply that the failure of space deterrence is acceptable, making space an environment that some PLA officers might see as safe for escalation.

The PLA's Turn Through 2020: More Proactive Behavior and Growing Risk Tolerance

From the mid-2010s through 2020, the PLA appeared to grow still more comfortable with the risk of escalation and uncertainty of crisis or conflict driven by an impetus to be more proactive in shaping China's security environment. As of 2020, PLA and Chinese civilian documents appeared to converge on the PLA's need to take more proactive military measures in China's external affairs coupled with a growing tolerance for risk from CCP leaders. Although no publicly available documents demonstrate the same point in space, PLA thinking on space operations almost certainly continues those trends seen in broader PLA thought and, thus, indicate a growing proclivity toward escalatory behavior in space.

The PLA's trend of becoming more proactive in shaping China's security environment originated from a 2016 directive from CCP General Secretary Xi Jinping, which drove a significant shift in PLA thinking about the use of force by introducing what official PLA media called a "new national security concept" that would "integrate planning for war preparation and termination, for deterrence and warfighting, and for military operations in war as well as non-war military activities."[80] According to official PLA media, this tightening alignment between the PLA's peacetime operations and its wartime missions serves to clarify China's redlines surrounding CCP interests (referred to as "bottom-line thinking") and to more proactively shape international environments in service of CCP objectives.[81] The importance of more proactive PLA force employment cannot be overstated. The official media explanation indicates that it entails "getting rid of the pattern of passive responses in national security maintenance" and, separately, "taking the initiative to break the situation, accumulate strategic advantages, and actively lead a transformation of the security situation in a direction favorable to China."[82]

---

[78] The principle that operations that do not threaten humanity are safe for escalation is an enduring piece of PLA thought. Reviewing the 2001 *Science of Military Strategy*, career intelligence officer Lonnie Henley assessed that "no conflict is likely to escalate to a point where national survival or millions of lives are at stake," and as a result, "Chinese writers almost seem to think these factors make the world safe for war" (Henley, 2007, p. 101).

[79] Zhou, Fu, and Wang, 2015, p. 52.

[80] Yang Ying [杨颖], "What Is the Purpose of Using Military Force in Peacetime?" ["和平时期军事力量运用, 目的在哪里?"], *China Military Online*, November 17, 2016.

[81] Yang, 2016.

[82] Yang, 2016.

Xi's guidance for the PLA to take more proactive measures has important implications for the PLA's approach to escalation. Key is the official media explanation that PLA operations prior to Xi's 2016 directive composed a pattern of passive response that maintained national security rather than forward-leaning efforts to secure political objectives.[83] This criticism likely referenced, among other aspects of PLA operational guidance, the paradigm of war control that emphasized cautious and precise assessments supporting bespoke operations.

Xi's guidance almost certainly dismissed the PLA and its prior way of practicing war control as too cautious. This is especially clear from a new generation of PLA PME, such as the 2017 and 2020 editions of the *Science of Military Strategy* published by the PLA NDU.[84] PLA thinking clearly evolved over the two editions to shed apprehension and embrace the uncertainty inherent within proactive efforts to shape China's security environment. Most importantly, although the 2017 *Science of Military Strategy* continued to refer throughout its text to the PLA's need to "control crisis" [控制危机], the 2020 edition referred instead to the PLA's requirement to "manage and control crisis" [管控危机], demonstrating a growing willingness to cope with—and actively shape—uncertainty arising from crisis situations.[85] Writing in the midst of this transition in 2018, PLA Army Service Academy [陆军勤务学院] researcher Zhou Ruochong emphasized similar proactivity when he argued that Xi's guidance following the 19th Party Congress in 2017 includes recognizing that "facing a crisis is not terrifying; what is truly terrifying is ignoring that a crisis might occur at any time and doing nothing when the crisis arrives."[86] Similarly, leading Chinese civilian scholarship also began describing CCP leadership as becoming increasingly interested in "seizing the initiative and taking some risks," reflecting growing tolerance for risk among the PLA's political leaders.[87]

Proactivity and Risk in Space

The shifts in PLA discourse reveal a military becoming more proactive in international affairs and more willing to accept escalation risk because of its proactive measures, pursuant to guidance from Xi. Although any updates to the 2013 PLA PME on space operations have not been made publicly available, open-source Chinese scholarship suggests that the broader trends of growing proactivity and

---

[83] Yang, 2016.

[84] This section identifies contrasts between the 2017 and 2020 editions of the *Science of Military Strategy* published by NDU and the 2001 and 2013 editions published by AMS. Although each edition has different authors and the recent editions have a different publisher, all are prominent PME textbooks summarizing top-level PLA views on military strategy. Given the prominent role each book has had in PLA officer education, these texts are likely aligned with PLA doctrine or policy and can be used to identify shifts in emphasis in PLA views of military strategy.

[85] Xiao, 2020, p. 111; Marcus Clay and Roderick Lee, "Unmasking the Devil in the Chinese Details: A Study Note on the *Science of Military Strategy 2020*," China Aerospace Studies Institute, January 24, 2022.

[86] Zhou Ruochong [周若冲], "Adapt to the Requirements of the Times by Improving Our Ability to Manage and Control Crises" ["适应时代要求提升管控危机能力"], *PLA Daily*, April 12, 2018.

[87] Zhang Yuyan [张宇燕], "An Integrated Approach to Development and Security: Grasping the Development Initiative" ["统筹发展和安全 把握发展主动权"], *Aisixiang*, January 15, 2021. The CCP's pivot toward taking more proactive actions has a wide range of drivers, likely including accumulating more power and tools needed to shape its security environment and CCP leaders' reprioritization of protecting the Party's economic development interests and security interests. For more on this development, see Howard Wang, "'Security Is a Prerequisite for Development': Consensus-Building Toward a New Top Priority in the Chinese Communist Party," *Journal of Contemporary China*, Vol. 32, No. 142, 2022.

risk tolerance extend to PLA thinking on escalation in space. Some research by PLA scholars appears to advocate for more forceful deterrence operations in space. For example, one set of researchers criticized the messaging around China's 2007 direct ascent anti-satellite test, asserting issues of classification mitigated what would otherwise be a "comprehensive and systematic psychological attack," and as a result the test "has yet to form a powerful shock" to adversary senses.[88] Other researchers, including AMS researcher Li Ruijing, described the importance of offensive space operations extending well into the future by asserting that "in the future of space warfare, attacking before the opponent does remains the most important way to strike."[89]

Although the specific operations comprising a more proactive and risk-accepting approach to space deterrence have yet to be seen, PLA discourse indicates the PLA has operationalized new guidance to take more proactive and assertive actions in general while accepting higher levels of escalation risk that might arise as consequence. In 2020, for example, the PLA simultaneously escalated its operations in its periphery, undertaking more coercive operations in the East China Sea, the South China Sea, and around Taiwan while also provoking a lethal clash with India, which Kurt Campbell and Mira Rapp-Hooper characterized as a "highly unusual full-court press."[90] The PLA of 2020 and beyond is more likely to undertake coercive activities and accept the risk of escalation with the United States than it was a decade prior. Although this more risk-accepting mindset was most visible in domains other than space, future PLA space operations could follow the same trend, particularly as Chinese space capabilities evolve.

China Dismisses Crisis Communications with the United States

The PLA's mounting assertiveness and growing risk tolerance in its external operations are particularly destabilizing for crisis stability in the context of Beijing's sustained disinterest in institutionalized crisis communications with the United States. The PLA has a well-established record of declining to participate in U.S.-China crisis communications, though CCP leaders have pursued similar mechanisms with other countries.[91] PLA scholarship suggests this discrepancy might arise from a Chinese perspective that the United States and China have fundamentally divergent interests, and crises arising between the two countries are the results of core incompatibilities that cannot be addressed with communications channels.

Despite the creation of a Washington-Beijing hotline in 1998, Chinese leaders were slow to respond to U.S. crisis outreach in 1999 following the United States' accidental bombing of the Chinese embassy in Belgrade and in 2001 following a collision between a Chinese jet and a U.S. EP-3

---

88 Wu and Ling, 2019.

89 Pan Chen [潘晨] and Li Ruijing [李瑞景], "Offense and Defense Approaches to the Future of Space Warfare" ["未来太空战的攻防之道"], *Science in 24 Hours* [科学 24 小时], No. 9, 2020.

90 Kurt Campbell and Mira Rapp-Hooper, "China Is Done Biding Its Time," *Foreign Affairs*, July 15, 2020.

91 For thorough accounts of China's crisis communication and signaling activities, see Yun Sun, "Why China Won't Talk with America's Military," *Foreign Affairs*, July 21, 2023; Scott W. Harold, Nathan Beauchamp-Mustafaga, and Soo Kim, *Assessing the Prospects for Great Power Cooperation in the Indo-Pacific*, RAND Corporation, RR-A597-2, 2023; Beauchamp-Mustafaga et al., 2021.

reconnaissance aircraft.[92] Similarly, during then–Speaker of the House Nancy Pelosi's visit to Taiwan in August 2022, Chinese officials and official media repeatedly characterized the event as a "crisis."[93] Despite their assessment, PLA leaders did not answer repeated calls from U.S. Secretary of Defense (SECDEF) Lloyd Austin and Chairman of the Joint Chiefs of Staff (CJCS) General Mark Milley who were attempting to alleviate crisis tensions.[94] Chinese leaders again reinforced this pattern of behavior during the United States' February 2023 strike on a Chinese spy balloon overflying the continental United States. Austin attempted to contact Chinese Minister of National Defense Wei Fenghe through a crisis hotline, but the Chinese side did not respond to the call.[95] The two countries established a "space hotline" in 2015, but no indicators currently suggest that Chinese leaders will be more inclined to use this hotline in times of crisis.[96] A brief history of such communications is outlined in Table 3.2.

Table 3.2. A Brief History of U.S.-China Crisis Communications

Year	Description
1989	President Bush is unable to reach CCP leader Deng Xiaoping during the Tiananmen Square protests and massacre (known in China as the June Fourth Incident).
1998	U.S. and China establish a direct presidential communications link.
1999	CCP leader Jiang Zemin declines call from President Clinton for several days following the United States' accidental bombing of the Chinese embassy in Belgrade.
2001	U.S. Ambassador in Beijing is unable to contact China's foreign ministry for 12 hours after the collision of U.S. Navy and PLA aircraft.
2008	U.S. and China establish the Defense Telephone Link (DTL) between the U.S. Office of the Secretary of Defense and the PRC Zhongnanhai Telecommunications Directorate.[a]
2015	U.S. and China establish a space hotline between the U.S. Joint Space Operations Center and the Beijing Institute of Tracking and Telecommunications Technology.
2020	Deputy Assistant Secretary of Defense (DASD) for China and CJCS schedule and conduct secure calls with their PLA counterparts following PLA accusations of U.S. preparations to launch "October Surprise" attacks on Chinese interests.
2022	SECDEF and CJCS submit multiple requests for a call through the DTL regarding then–Speaker Pelosi's congressional delegation to Taiwan, but the PLA did not take action on the requests.

[92] Avery Goldstein, "First Things First: The Pressing Danger of Crisis Instability in U.S.-China Relations," *International Security*, Vol. 37, No. 4, 2013, p. 63.

[93] "Ministry of National Defense Spokesperson Wu Qian Makes a Statement on Pelosi's Visit to Taiwan," Xinhua, August 2, 2022; "Chinese Vice Foreign Minister Answers Questions on Pelosi's Taiwan Visit," Xinhua, August 10, 2022; "Some Facts About Pelosi's Visit to Taiwan," Xinhua, August 25, 2022.

[94] Lara Seligman and Alexander Ward, "Pentagon Chiefs' Calls to China Go Unanswered Amid Taiwan Crisis," *Politico*, August 5, 2022.

[95] Ellen Knickmeyer, "'It Just Rang': In Crises, US-China Hotline Goes Unanswered," Associated Press, February 10, 2023.

[96] Sam Jones, "US and China Set Up 'Space Hotline,'" *Financial Times*, November 20, 2015.

Year	Description
2023	February: SECDEF requests for a call via DTL to PLA Minister of National Defense Wei Fenghe go unanswered during Chinese spy balloon overflight of the continental United States. June: Secretary of State Anthony Blinken repeatedly raises the need for a military-to-military crisis communication line in meetings with CCP leaders, who reject the proposal.

SOURCES: Features information from Laura Kelly, "Xi Rejects US Offer to Set Up Military Crisis Hotline, Blinken Says," *The Hill*, June 19, 2023; Knickmeyer, 2023; Seligman and Ward, 2022; Office of the Chairman of the Joint Chiefs of Staff, "General Milley's Engagements with the People's Liberation Army Leaders," memorandum for the record, September 27, 2021, p. 6; Phelim Kine, "'Spiral Into Crisis': The U.S.-China Military Hotline Is Dangerously Broken," *Politico*, September 1, 2021; "China—Tiananmen Square—the U.S. Response," George & Barbara Bush Foundation, June 4, 2019; Jones, 2015; Agreement on the Establishment of a Secure Defense Telephone Link Between the Department of Defense, the United States of America and the Ministry of National Defense, the People's Republic of China, February 29, 2008; "Jiang Finally Takes Clinton's Call of Apology for Embassy Bombing," *Wall Street Journal*, May 15, 1999; DoD, *The United States Security Strategy for the East Asia-Pacific Region*, 1998, p. 34.
NOTE: PRC = People's Republic of China.
[a] The DTL is a secure telephone link facilitating voice communication between DoD and the Chinese Ministry of National Defense's Foreign Affairs Office, but it requires advance coordination to operate. The agreement establishing the DTL stipulates that the party initiating a request through the DTL must provide 48 hours' notice of the call and topics for conversation, and both sides must coordinate call times and topics in advance. Although either party might waive the 48-hour notice and request an immediate working-level call in a time of crisis, the other party is not required to accept this request (Agreement on the Establishment of a Secure Defense Telephone Link Between the Department of Defense, the United States of America and the Ministry of National Defense, the People's Republic of China, 2008, p. 5).

Notably, in 2022, the Chinese Ministry of Foreign Affairs spokesperson stated, "China is willing to establish a long-term communications mechanism with the United States proceeding from maintaining the safety of Chinese astronauts and China's [Tiangong] space station."[97] This statement followed a Chinese claim that China's Tiangong space station and two Starlink satellites were involved in a close approach that the Chinese side considered to be dangerous.[98] Public reports do not clarify whether this would be a political crisis communications mechanism useful for clarifying security intentions or a technical communications mechanism between operators to ensure day-to-day operational safety. Although the Ministry of Foreign Affairs' statement implies that communications mechanisms could further develop beyond the initial and limited focus on protecting China's space station, there is little evidence to suggest that China will allow the notional dialogue to eventually include U.S. crisis communication priorities.[99] In fact, Chinese officials have repeatedly used dialogue with the United States in bad faith. Former Assistant Secretary of Defense for Indo-Pacific Security

[97] Ministry of Foreign Affairs, "Foreign Ministry Spokesperson Zhao Lijian's Regular Press Conference for February 10, 2022" ["2022 年 2 月 10 日外交部发言人赵立坚主持例行记者会"], February 10, 2022.

[98] Ministry of Foreign Affairs, 2022.

[99] China's Ministry of Foreign Affairs primarily uses international dialogue for one-way communication to clarify CCP demands without offering its diplomats any flexibility to accommodate interlocutors. Chinese diplomats are often not involved in CCP policy processes to ensure that the information they can share with foreign interlocutors adheres to approved talking points. This practice has sharply limited what U.S. diplomats can hope to gain from established communications mechanisms with China's Ministry of Foreign Affairs (Peter Martin, *China's Civilian Army*, Oxford University Press, 2021, pp. 53–54).

Affairs Randy Schriver assessed that Chinese officers at U.S.-PLA military exchanges tended to be "military intelligence officials and political warfare professionals" whose missions were likely not to engage in substantive cooperation with U.S. officials, and he further characterized other dialogues, such as the U.S.-China Strategic and Economic Dialogues, as ones in which Chinese leaders "promote their status as a global power without agreeing to bear any of the real responsibilities and burdens of a relationship."[100]

Some of these missed or delayed communications might be due to the structure of China's national security bureaucracy. At a public 2023 event, former DASD for China Chad Sbragia assessed Chinese external communications systems to be immature and unable to rapidly respond in a crisis. According to Sbragia, connectivity is not the challenge in U.S.-China crisis communications. Rather, the procedural question of who on the Chinese side is authorized to pick up and speak over a crisis hotline has yet to be resolved, feeding Chinese reticence to use such a mechanism. Furthermore, Sbragia assessed that crisis engagements "have to be vetted by all domains of their security apparatus," presenting a cumbersome approval burden that imposes time lags on PLA responses in rapidly developing crises.[101]

Crisis communications have not appeared to substantially reassure Chinese leaders when they did occur. Notably, in September 2020, PLA officials stated Chinese leaders' belief that the Trump administration might initiate a military crisis with China as an "October Surprise" ahead of the 2020 U.S. presidential election. Despite repeated outreach from Austin and Milley to reassure their PLA counterparts no such crisis would occur, the PLA declined to participate in a December 2020 dialogue with U.S. Indo-Pacific Command and did not reduce heightened operational readiness levels until January 30, 2021, after the Biden administration had taken office.[102]

Some PLA research suggests that China takes a unique approach to the United States in its crisis communication policy because of long-standing and irreconcilable differences between U.S. and CCP interests. The 2013 *China Military Science* article authored by professors in the PLA NDU Crisis Management Center emphasizes that the mechanism by which crisis communications mechanisms prevent uncontrolled escalation is by aiding the understanding of each party's intent in the crisis. To that end, the authors advocated for maintaining communications through a diversity of channels in a crisis and further urged that communications channels "should not be cut off completely unless a special situation arises."[103] Where intentions are known, however, such as when military crises arise as the "inevitable result of a conflict of national interest that has gone unresolved over a long period of time," then the authors claimed escalation becomes inevitable—regardless of the presence of crisis communications—as one or both parties to the crisis use the situation to improve their strategic position.[104] Chinese leaders might not prioritize crisis dialogue with the United States if they believe

[100] U.S.-China Economic and Security Review Commission, "China's Military Diplomacy and Overseas Security Activities," hearing transcript, January 26, 2023; Bill Gertz, "U.S., China Strategic and Economic Dialogue Criticized," *Washington Free Beacon*, July 16, 2013.

[101] United States Institute of Peace, "U.S.-China Crisis Communications in Dire Straits," June 13, 2023.

[102] Office of the Chairman of the Joint Chiefs of Staff, 2021, pp. 6–7.

[103] Zhao and Zhao, 2013.

[104] Zhao and Zhao, 2013.

they have a clear understanding of U.S. intentions or if they believe they will not learn much useful information about U.S. intentions from crisis dialogue.

The PLA might stiffen its resolve against crisis communication as escalation continues and war appears more likely. The NDU researchers are careful to caveat that "various parties involved in a crisis can still find a point of balance through bargaining *other than in a crisis that is directed toward war*" (emphasis added), which the authors defined as a crisis that is manufactured by one party to achieve its political objective and in which the country has made the determination to go to war before provoking the crisis.[105] As a future crisis with the United States grows more severe, PLA leaders might grow increasingly convinced that continued escalation and the relative failure of PLA efforts to deter the United States indicate that the United States manufactured a crisis for the purposes of resolving long-term conflict between the two countries through military force. Sbragia shared a similar assessment, noting the United States' repeated calls for establishing a crisis communications mechanism "frightens the Chinese off," implying that the PLA might believe the United States would feel more freedom of action to precipitate or escalate a crisis if it had a mechanism to de-escalate.[106] In such a case, the PLA would likely not assess that it can clarify intentions or find a point of balance through crisis communication, rendering such communications moot.

[105] Zhao and Zhao, 2013.

[106] United States Institute of Peace, 2023.

Chapter 4

Conclusion: China's Pathologies Drive Crisis Escalation in Space

The PLA views the United States with a profound sense of threat. Chinese leaders harbor deep suspicions of the United States, which they view as technologically superior and rapaciously implementing hegemony-maintenance strategies. As a result, Chinese leaders have inflated threat perceptions of the United States and are unlikely to cooperate with U.S. officials to arrest unintended crisis escalation. Instead, CCP leaders are more likely to direct the PLA to compete rather than cooperate with the United States and USSF.

To prosecute competitive strategies against the United States, the PLA is likely to adopt aggressive deterrence operations in the space domain, up to and including the use of lethal force. The PLA's approach to deterrence and escalation in space prioritizes securing political objectives over avoiding conflict, and Beijing could initiate conflict activities if it judged that the political risk of inaction exceeded the military risk. The PLA's shift toward greater risk acceptance in its PME likely makes space a riskier operating environment for all countries operating in this domain. In conjunction with the CCP's enduring suspicion of U.S. intentions, this policy of risk-accepting behavior and reluctance to cooperate on U.S. initiatives might result in unintended escalation with the United States.

Three key findings and implications arise from this analysis, each discussed in greater detail below. First, the PLA's suspicions of U.S. intentions are an enduring aspect of U.S.-China relations, and U.S. space operators looking to convey messages to the PLA will need to account for that suspicion. Second, CCP leader direction and PLA PME between 2013 and 2020 have pushed the PLA toward a more proactive and risk-accepting posture, likely composing a new normal of heightened friction in day-to-day space operations. Still, the PLA's risk-accepting behavior will advance rather than undermine CCP political objectives, and PLA proactivity is not likely to reach a point at which it risks politically sensitive missions (such as Taiwan). Finally, the CCP's inflated threat perceptions of the United States leave little room for cooperative crisis control between the PLA and U.S. military, and U.S. officials managing a crisis in space will likely need to do so without the support of or sustained communication with their Chinese counterparts.

PLA's Enduring Suspicions

This report identifies two key trends in the PLA's approach to U.S.-China crisis stability in space. First, Chinese analysts, including PLA researchers, have consistently expressed intense suspicions of U.S. intentions and view U.S. space policy from the Eisenhower administration through at least the Trump administration as pursuing hegemony in space. Second, the PLA has grown increasingly proactive and risk tolerant in its approach to escalation by seeking to "effectively shape the situation" and "manage and control crises" in place of what Chinese state media dismissed as its passive response of prior behavior.[107]

These trends are likely to persist. The identified PLA perceptions are not specific to any individual U.S. presidential administration and continue well beyond 2020. In 2021, researchers from AMS and the SSF's Aerospace Engineering University assessed that the U.S. military has "integrated space combat into its joint operations and is eager to give space warfare a try," thereby "enormously increasing the risk a war might break out in space."[108] In 2023, the director of China's Ministry of State Security–affiliated China Institutes of Contemporary International Relations Arms Control Research Center argued that the United States' "bravado" in space has increased the risk of space war, and as a result of U.S. policies, "the current risk of a space war has far surpassed that of the Cold War."[109] As of 2023, the PLA also continues to urge its rank and file to adopt a proactive and risk-tolerant approach to the United States across the spectrum of conflict. Authoritative PLA state media and AMS-published PME reiterate that the PLA must continue to "effectively shape the situation" and "manage and control crises," reinforcing the proactive turn in the PLA's approach to escalation.[110]

Escalation Might Be Provocative but Politically Controlled

The PLA's push to proactively shape its strategic environment indicates that USSF will face a bellicose PLA eager to assert itself in space during peacetime, though the PLA remains unlikely to escalate in a way that risks its political imperatives. Particularly because PLA leaders appear to anticipate low costs for escalating in space, USSF should anticipate that PLA provocations in peacetime likely comprise a new normal in day-to-day space operations that involve China. Still, the PLA's proactive steps and higher risk tolerance remain subordinate to political decisionmaking. In interpreting PLA messaging, USSF operators should anticipate that the PLA is not likely to take proactive, escalatory steps in a crisis if those steps undermine its ability to prosecute politically imperative missions, such as a war over Taiwan.

The PLA's wide range of deterrent activities, including kinetic strikes on adversary systems, might also confuse its messaging with excess aggression. For example, the most escalatory deterrence operation in space noted in the *Lectures* is the "overawing space strike," which can entail limited-scale, kinetic initial strikes to hard kill U.S. space assets.[111] Although such an operation would likely indicate that the PLA perceives itself to be in a pitched moment of crisis, its categorization as a deterrent

---

[107] Yang, 2016.

[108] Li Meihong [李美红] and Tang Yafeng [汤亚锋], "The United States' Militarization of Space Has Moved Many Countries to Concern" ["美太空军事化动作引各国担忧"], *PLA Daily*, October 14, 2021.

[109] Guo Xiaobing [郭晓兵], "The U.S. Plays Up Space War, Highlighting Its Cold War Mentality" ["美国渲染太空战凸显冷战思维"], *People's Daily*, April 13, 2023.

[110] "Deepen Preparations for Military Struggle and Create a New Situation in Military Building" ["深入推進軍事斗爭准備 開創部隊建設新局面"], *PLA Daily*, July 31, 2023; "Introduction to the Main Contents of the *Selected Important Documents on the Military Work of the Communist Party of China*," Xinhua, July 30, 2023.

[111] Jiang, 2013, pp. 127–128.

operation means that CCP leaders might not have made a decision to go to war. In such a case, USSF operators and DoD leaders must be prepared to navigate this ambiguity in CCP intent.

Few Prospects for Cooperative Crisis Control

Moreover, U.S. officials have few policy options—and fewer good policy options—for avoiding or managing crises with China in space. Inflated CCP and PLA views of U.S. intentions as hegemonic and capabilities as unfettered leave little room for confidence-building between the United States and China, particularly because the PLA appears unable or unwilling to establish responsive crisis communications and further embraces increasingly risk-tolerant approaches toward escalation. Critically, PLA researchers see crisis communications mechanisms as leverage-bearing tools. Because Chinese leaders see the United States as prosecuting hegemony-maintaining strategies against China, Chinese leaders tend to interpret U.S.-led efforts to establish crisis communications mechanisms or broader space norms as tools to control China's behavior. Therefore, Chinese leaders believe it is not in China's interest to engage with the United States. U.S. officials responsible for managing crisis dynamics with China can reasonably expect a limited decision space and unabated suspicion from Chinese counterparts leading up to and during a crisis.

Equally concerning is the PLA's apparent resistance to U.S. attempts to establish strategic guardrails for space activities in peacetime. PLA researchers appear convinced that the United States is a rapacious hegemon intent on undermining Chinese interests in the teeth of what these researchers see as undeniable trends of "the East is rising; the West is declining."[112] The open-source literature reviewed for this report, although limited, consistently shows that this perspective extends into PLA assessments of U.S.-China dynamics in space. PLA researchers find that U.S. space capabilities and partnerships are highly sophisticated and coalesced to achieve a singular objective of maintaining "absolute space superiority" to extend U.S. hegemony over Chinese interests.[113] As U.S.-China strategic competition intensified over the decade from 2013 through 2023, the PLA's approach to escalation dynamics in space very likely aligned with broader PLA-wide trends to more assertively employ force to shape China's security environment, including at the cost of accepting higher levels of risk.[114]

These suspicions pose a complex challenge to U.S. officials looking to establish crisis-averting behaviors or mechanisms for space in peacetime. Chinese leaders' perceptions of the United States as fundamentally threatening Chinese national rejuvenation foster a tendency to deny the U.S. government its preferred strategic stability guardrails to reduce tensions in a crisis.[115] Chinese leaders view the broader U.S. strategic intent as suppressing China in competitive domains—including space—and, therefore, these leaders are likely to perceive U.S.-led attempts to establish bilateral agreements in space as ultimately serving a goal of maintaining U.S. hegemony to the detriment of

---

[112] Tian, 2023.

[113] Fan and Gong, 2016.

[114] Yang, 2016.

[115] See discussions of the U.S. pursuit of strategic guardrails in Susan Thornton, "Prospects for U.S.-China Strategic Stability and Crisis Management," Stimson Center, August 2, 2021; Richard Maude, "Why China Relations Need the Guardrails on Them," Australian Financial Review, April 14, 2023.

Chinese interests. PLA sources do not reveal a consideration of U.S. approaches as offering mutually beneficial advantages, a necessary prerequisite for durable bilateral strategic guardrails.

These writings reveal a deeply suspicious and competitive view of the U.S. approach to establish norms to avoid escalation in space. It is highly likely that this competitive mindset would preclude China from acceding to agreements on space norms that were not initiated by China. Yet, similarly, any norms proposed by China would likely carry the baseline competitive intent of limiting ongoing U.S. military space activities that China perceives as weaponization, making them unlikely to be palatable to U.S. policymakers. The *Lectures* states this directly when it instructs

> by following the path of international cooperation in order to develop your own space strengths, and through signing bilateral or multilateral international space conventions and agreements, it is not only possible to quickly strengthen your own space military power, but it is also possible to restrain to a certain extent your opponent's actions for attacking your own spacecraft.[116]

Thus, the PLA's consistent resistance to U.S. efforts to build strategic stability precludes outright cooperation in mitigating the variables that make unintended crisis escalation in space ever more likely. Without the direct means for arresting unintended crisis escalation in space, U.S. officials responsible for managing U.S.-China crises in space will likely need to adapt to a limited decision space with little communication to achieve a version of stability that Chinese leaders will tolerate. Moreover, U.S. officials will likely need to do so without expectations of cooperation with the PLA. To that end, U.S. officials should avoid investing costly efforts or making significant policy concessions to establish crisis communications mechanisms with the PLA. Given the CCP history of aversion to crisis communications with the United States, PLA overtures to discuss such mechanisms might not be made in good faith. Nor are communications mechanisms focusing on safety likely to be upgraded into crisis communications affecting security. Instead, such overtures will likely be efforts to bait the United States into sinking time and energy into endless negotiations.

[116] Jiang, 2013, p. 38.

Abbreviations

AMS	Academy of Military Science
CASC	China Aerospace Science and Technology Corporation
CCP	Chinese Communist Party
CJCS	Chairman of the Joint Chiefs of Staff
DASD	Deputy Assistant Secretary of Defense
DoD	U.S. Department of Defense
DTL	Defense Telephone Link
JLSF	Joint Logistics Support Force
NDU	National Defense University
NUDT	National University of Defense Technology
PLA	People's Liberation Army
PME	professional military education
SECDEF	Secretary of Defense
SSF	Strategic Support Force
USSF	U.S. Space Force

Bibliography

Academy of Military Science All-Military Military Terminology Committee [全军军事术语管理委员会军事科学院], *Junyu* [军语], Academy of Military Science Publishing House [军事科学出版社出版], 2011.

Agreement on the Establishment of a Secure Defense Telephone Link Between the Department of Defense, the United States of America and the Ministry of National Defense, the People's Republic of China, February 29, 2008.

Air Force Space Command Public Affairs, "Schriever Wargame Concludes," Schriever Space Force Base, December 18, 2015.

Baucom, Donald R., "The Rise and Fall of Brilliant Pebbles," *Journal of Social, Political and Economic Studies*, Vol. 29, No. 2, Summer 2004.

Beauchamp-Mustafaga, Nathan, "Dare to Face the 'Strong Enemy 强敌': How Xi Jinping Has Made the PLA Talk About the United States," *Sinocism*, March 4, 2021.

Beauchamp-Mustafaga, Nathan, "Exploring Chinese Thinking on Deterrence in the Not-So-New Space and Cyber Domains," in *Modernizing Deterrence: How China Coerces, Compels, and Deters*, National Bureau of Asian Research, 2023.

Beauchamp-Mustafaga, Nathan, Derek Grossman, Kristen Gunness, Michael S. Chase, Marigold Black, and Natalia D. Simmons-Thomas, *Deciphering Chinese Deterrence Signalling in the New Era: An Analytic Framework and Seven Case Studies*, RAND Corporation, RR-A1074-1, 2021. As of July 11, 2023: https://www.rand.org/pubs/research_reports/RRA1074-1.html

Bingen, Kari A., Kaitlyn Johnson, Makena Young, and John Raymond, *Space Threat Assessment 2023*, Center for Strategic and International Studies, 2023.

Blanc, Alexis A., Nathan Beauchamp-Mustafaga, Khrystyna Holynska, M. Scott Bond, and Stephen J. Flanagan, *Chinese and Russian Perceptions of and Responses to U.S. Military Activities in the Space Domain*, RAND Corporation, RR-A1835-1, 2022. As of July 11, 2023: https://www.rand.org/pubs/research_reports/RRA1835-1.html

Burke, Kristin, "Understanding China's Space Leading Small Groups—The Best Way to Determine the PLA's Influence," China Aerospace Studies Institute, July 2022.

Campbell, Kurt M., and Mira Rapp-Hooper, "China Is Done Biding Its Time," *Foreign Affairs*, July 15, 2020.

Chen Yunlei [陈云雷], Li Xianglong [李向龙], and Wang Xinxin [王鑫鑫], "Research on the Trend of Military Application of Satellite Internet in the United States and Its Impact" ["美国卫星互联网军事应用趋势及其影响研"], *Aerodynamic Missile Journal* [飞航导弹], No. 2, 2021.

"China, Philippines Pledge More Efforts to Maintain Peace, Stability in South China Sea," Xinhua, October 30, 2018.

"China—Tiananmen Square—the U.S. Response," George & Barbara Bush Foundation, June 4, 2019.

"China's Space Station Tiangong Enters New Phase of Application, Development," Xinhua, December 10, 2022.

"Chinese Vice Foreign Minister Answers Questions on Pelosi's Taiwan Visit," Xinhua, August 10, 2022.

Clay, Marcus, and Roderick Lee, "Unmasking the Devil in the Chinese Details: A Study Note on the *Science of Military Strategy 2020*," China Aerospace Studies Institute, January 24, 2022.

Cloud, David S., and Austin Ramzy, "China-Brokered Deal Between Iran, Saudi Arabia Marks a New Middle East," *Wall Street Journal*, March 11, 2023.

Communist Network [共产党员网], "1. Realizing the Chinese Dream of the Great Rejuvenation of the Chinese Nation" ["一、实现中华民族伟大复兴的中国梦"], undated.

"Deepen Preparations for Military Struggle and Create a New Situation in Military Building" ["深入推進軍事斗爭准備 開創部隊建設新局面"], *PLA Daily*, July 31, 2023.

Defense Intelligence Agency, *Challenges to Security in Space: Space Reliance in an Era of Competition and Expansion*, 2022.

DoD—*See* U.S. Department of Defense.

Fan Gaoyue [樊高月] and Gong Xuping [宫旭平], "The Development and Evolution of American Space Strategic Thought (Part 1)" ["美国太空战略思想的发展与演变(上)"], *National Defense* [国防], No. 2, 2016a.

Fan Gaoyue [樊高月] and Gong Xuping [宫旭平], "The Development and Evolution of American Space Strategic Thought (Part 2)" ["美国太空战略思想的发展与演变(上)"], *National Defense* [国防], No. 3, 2016b.

Flores, Helen, "Philippines, China to Open More Lines of Communication," *Philippine Star*, April 23, 2023.

"Full Text: China's Space Program: A 2021 Perspective," Xinhua, January 28, 2022.

Gertz, Bill, "U.S., China Strategic and Economic Dialogue Criticized," *Washington Free Beacon*, July 16, 2013.

Ghoshal, Devjyot, "India, China to Withdraw from Disputed Border Area by Monday," Reuters, September 9, 2022.

Goldstein, Avery, "First Things First: The Pressing Danger of Crisis Instability in U.S.-China Relations," *International Security*, Vol. 37, No. 4, 2013.

Guo Jun [郭俊], "Viewing the Construction of U.S. Space Deterrent Force from the 'Schriever' Exercise" ["'从施里弗' 演习看美军太空威慑力量构建"], *National Defense Science and Technology* [国防科技], Vol. 36, No. 1, February 2015.

Guo Wenbo [苟文波], Luo Wei [罗威], and Bi Chenglong [毕成龙], "Analysis of U.S. Space Training and Readiness Command" ["美军太空训练与战备司令部浅析"], *Aerospace China* [中国航天], No. 11, 2022.

Guo Xiaobing [郭晓兵], "The U.S. Plays Up Space War, Highlighting Its Cold War Mentality" ["美国渲染太空战凸显冷战思维"], *People's Daily*, April 13, 2023.

Harold, Scott W., Nathan Beauchamp-Mustafaga, and Soo Kim, *Assessing the Prospects for Great Power Cooperation in the Indo-Pacific*, RAND Corporation, RR-A597-2, 2023. As of March 7, 2024: https://www.rand.org/pubs/research_reports/RRA597-2.html

Henley, Lonnie D., "Evolving Chinese Concepts of War Control and Escalation Management," in Michael D. Swaine, Andrew N. D. Yang, and Evan S. Medeiros with Oriana Skylar Mastro, eds., *Assessing the Threat: The Chinese Military and Taiwan's Security*, Carnegie Endowment for International Peace, 2007.

"In Test, Military Hits Satellite Using a Laser," *New York Times*, October 21, 1997.

India Ministry of External Affairs, "Joint Press Statement—Meeting of External Affairs Minister and the Foreign Minister of China (September 10, 2020)," September 10, 2020.

"Introduction to the Main Contents of the *Selected Important Documents on the Military Work of the Communist Party of China*," Xinhua, July 30, 2023.

"Jiang Finally Takes Clinton's Call of Apology for Embassy Bombing," *Wall Street Journal*, May 15, 1999.

Jiang Lianju [姜连举], ed., *Lectures on the Science of Space Operations* [空间作战学教程], Military Science Press [军事科学出版社], 2013.

Jones, Sam, "US and China Set Up 'Space Hotline,'" *Financial Times*, November 20, 2015.

Kan, Shirley A., "U.S.-China Military Contacts: Issues for Congress," Congressional Research Service, December 12, 2014.

Kelly, Laura, "Xi Rejects US Offer to Set Up Military Crisis Hotline, Blinken Says," *The Hill*, June 19, 2023.

Kine, Phelim, "'Spiral Into Crisis': The U.S.-China Military Hotline Is Dangerously Broken," *Politico*, September 1, 2021.

Knickmeyer, Ellen, "'It Just Rang': In Crises, US-China Hotline Goes Unanswered," Associated Press, February 10, 2023.

Koren, Marina, "China's Growing Ambitions in Space," *The Atlantic*, January 23, 2017.

Langeland, Krista, and Derek Grossman, *Tailoring Deterrence for China in Space*, RAND Corporation, RR-A943-1, 2021. As of March 7, 2024: https://www.rand.org/pubs/research_reports/RRA943-1.html

Li Meihong [李美红] and Tang Yafeng [汤亚锋], "The United States' Militarization of Space Has Moved Many Countries to Concern" ["美太空军事化动作引各国担忧"], *PLA Daily*, October 14, 2021.

Lo, Kinling, "China, Malaysia Seek to Resolve South China Sea Disputes with New Dialogue Mechanism," *South China Morning Post*, September 13, 2019.

Long Kun [龙坤], Zhu Qichao [朱启超], Chen Xi [陈曦], and Ma Ning [马宁] , "The Motivation, Characteristics and Influence of the Trump Administration's Space Defense Strategy Adjustment" ["特朗普政府太空防卫战略调整的动因, 特点与影响"], *National Defense Technology* [国防科技], Vol. 42, No. 4, 2021.

Martin, Peter, *China's Civilian Army*, Oxford University Press, 2021.

Maude, Richard, "Why China Relations Need the Guardrails on Them," Australian Financial Review, April 14, 2023.

Ministry of Foreign Affairs, "Foreign Ministry Spokesperson Zhao Lijian's Regular Press Conference for February 10, 2022" ["2022 年 2 月 10 日外交部发言人赵立坚主持例行记者会"], February 10, 2022.

"Ministry of National Defense Spokesperson Wu Qian Makes a Statement on Pelosi's Visit to Taiwan," Xinhua, August 2, 2022.

Office of the Chairman of the Joint Chiefs of Staff, "General Milley's Engagements with the People's Liberation Army Leaders," memorandum for the record, September 27, 2021.

O'Toole, Thomas, "Space Shuttle Succeeds in Laser Test," *Washington Post*, June 22, 1985.

Pan Chen [潘晨] and Li Ruijing [李瑞景], "Offense and Defense Approaches to the Future of Space Warfare" ["未来太空战的攻防之道"], *Science in 24 Hours* [科学 24 小时], No. 9, 2020.

Pancevski, Bojan, Laurence Norman, and Vivian Salama, "U.S. and Allies Look at Potential China Role in Ending Ukraine War," *Wall Street Journal*, May 7, 2023.

Peng Guangqian and Yao Youzhi, eds., *The Science of Military Strategy*, official English-language translation of the 2001 Chinese edition, Military Science Press, 2005.

Provincial Health Commission of Hubei Province, "'New, Progressive, Real'—Analysis of Key Words in the New Development State" ["'新, 进, 实' 一新发展阶段的关键词浅析"], January 7, 2021.

Ren Changsheng [任长胜] and Deng Yunan [邓雨楠], "CASC Held the 2021 New Employee Initiation Training Opening Ceremony" ["航天科技集团召开 2021 年新员工入职培训开班式"], *China Space News* [中国航天报], August 6, 2021.

Rolland, Nadège, *China's Vision for a New World Order*, National Bureau of Asian Research, 2022.

Ruan Jianping, Deng Kaifan, and Wang Jiamin, "Building Guardrails: Crisis Management in China-US Competition," *China Quarterly of International Strategic Studies*, Vol. 8, No. 2, 2022.

Schelling, Thomas C., "Confidence in Crisis," *International Security*, Vol. 8, No. 4, Spring 1984.

Schelling, Thomas C., *Arms and Influence*, reprint, Yale University Press, 2008.

Seligman, Lara, and Alexander Ward, "Pentagon Chiefs' Calls to China Go Unanswered Amid Taiwan Crisis," *Politico*, August 5, 2022.

Shou Xiaosong [寿晓松], ed., *Science of Military Strategy*, Academy of Military Science Press, 2013.

"Some Facts About Pelosi's Visit to Taiwan," Xinhua, August 25, 2022.

State Council Information Office [国务院新闻办公室], *China's National Defense in the New Era* [新时代的中国国防], July 24, 2019.

Su Feng [粟锋] and Xu Nengwu [徐能武], "Countermeasures and Developmental Trends of the US Defense Space Force Based on the Interpretation of the US *Defense Space Strategy* in 2020" ["美国国防太空力量发展的动向及应对—基于对美国 2020 年《国防太空战略》的解读"], *National Defense Technology* [国防科技], Vol. 42, No. 3, 2021.

Sun, Yun, "Why China Won't Talk with America's Military," *Foreign Affairs*, July 21, 2023.

Thornton, Susan, "Prospects for U.S.-China Strategic Stability and Crisis Management," Stimson Center, August 2, 2021.

Tian Peiyan [田培炎], "Deeply Study and Understand Xi Jinping Thought on Socialism with Chinese Characteristics for a New Era" ["深学细悟习近平新时代中国特色社会主义思想"], *People's Daily*, July 4, 2023.

Tobin, Daniel, "How Xi Jinping's 'New Era' Should Have Ended U.S. Debate on Beijing's Ambitions," testimony before the U.S.-China Economic and Security Review Commission hearing on *A 'China Model'? Beijing's Promotion of Alternative Global Norms and Standards*, March 13, 2020.

"Transcript: President Xi Jinping's Report to China's 2022 Party Congress," *Nikkei Asia*, October 18, 2022.

United States Institute of Peace, "U.S.-China Crisis Communications in Dire Straits," June 13, 2023.

U.S.-China Economic and Security Review Commission, *2021 Annual Report to Congress of the U.S.-China Economic and Security Review Commission*, 2021.

U.S.-China Economic and Security Review Commission, "China's Military Diplomacy and Overseas Security Activities," hearing transcript, January 26, 2023.

U.S. Department of Defense, *The United States Security Strategy for the East Asia-Pacific Region*, 1998.

U.S. Department of Defense, *Defense Space Strategy Summary*, June 2020.

Wang, Howard, "'Security Is a Prerequisite for Development': Consensus-Building Toward a New Top Priority in the Chinese Communist Party," *Journal of Contemporary China*, Vol. 32, No. 142, 2022.

Wang Xiang [王翔], "On the Latest Developments of U.S. and Russian Space Defense: Overview and Implications" ["美俄新一轮太空防务建设及启示"], *National Defense* [国防], No. 7, 2019.

Weeden, Brian, and Victoria Samson, eds., *Global Counterspace Capabilities: An Open Source Assessment*, Secure World Foundation, 2023.

Wu Ming [吴明] and Ling Shengyin [凌胜银], "Strategic Thinking on Strengthening Our Country's Space Deterrence Capability Construction" ["加强我国太空威慑能力建设的战略思考"], *China Military to Civilian* [中国军转民], No. 2, 2019.

Wu Yansheng [吴燕生], "Guided by General Secretary Xi Jinping's Important Exposition on Building China into a Space Power, Strive to Write a New Chapter in the Development of China's Space Industry" ["以习近平总书记关于建设航天强国重要论述为指引 奋力谱写航天事业发展新篇章"], *Party Building* [党建], June 21, 2022.

"Xi Jinping Earnestly Entrusts the Task of Building China into a Space Great Power," Xinhua, April 12, 2019.

"Xi Jinping Presides Over the First Meeting of the 20th Central National Security Commission and Emphasizes Accelerating the Modernization of a National Security System and Capabilities Such That a New Security Pattern Safeguards the New Development Pattern," Xinhua, May 30, 2023.

Xiao Tianliang [肖天亮], ed., *Science of Military Strategy (2020 Edition)*, [战略学 (2020 年修订)], National Defense University Press [国防大学出版社], 2020.

Xie Shanshan [谢珊珊], Wu Ling [吴灵], and Li Yun [李云], "Research and Analysis of the U.S. National Defense Space Strategy" ["美国《国防太空战略》研究分析"], *Aerospace China* [中国航天], No. 9, 2020.

Xu Nengwu [徐能武] and Huang Changyun [黄长云], "The Origin, Evolution and Development Trend of Space Arms Control from the Perspective of International Security" ["国际安全视角下太空军控的缘起，演进和发展动向"], *Diplomatic Review* [外交评论], No. 5, 2014.

Yang Ying [杨颖], "What Is the Purpose of Using Military Force in Peacetime?" ["和平时期军事力量运用，目的在哪里?"], *China Military Online*, November 17, 2016.

Yin Hang [尹航], Guo Su [郭谡], Wen Chaoran [温超然], Yang Chuang [杨闯], and Bi Peng [毕鹏], "Analysis of Development of US MALD and Coping Strategies" ["美微型空射诱饵武器发展分析与应对策略"], *Air & Space Defense* [空天防御] Vol. 2, No. 3, 2019.

Zhang Yuyan [张宇燕], "An Integrated Approach to Development and Security: Grasping the Development Initiative" ["统筹发展和安全 把握发展主动权"], *Aisixiang*, January 15, 2021.

Zhao Ziyu [赵子聿] and Zhao Jingfang [赵景芳], "On Control and Management of Military Crises" ["论军事危机的管控"], *China Military Science* [中国军事科学], No. 4, 2013.

Zhong Jing [仲晶], "Strategic Competition and Games in Space Are Becoming Increasingly Fierce" ["太空战略竞争与博弈日趋激烈"], *Academic Frontiers* [学术前沿], No. 8, 2020.

Zhou Lini [周黎妮], Fu Zhongli [傅中力], and Wang Shu [王姝], "Comparison Between Space Deterrence and Nuclear Deterrence" ["太空威慑与核威慑比较研究"], *National Defense Science & Technology* [国防科技], Vol. 36, No. 3, June 2015.

Zhou Ruochong [周若冲], "Adapt to the Requirements of the Times by Improving Our Ability to Manage and Control Crises" ["适应时代要求提升管控危机能力"], *PLA Daily*, April 12, 2018.